POEMS
FROM THE
HEART

BY JEAN MARIE NORMAN

A Book of
Life, Love, Loss & Laughter

◆ FriesenPress

One Printers Way
Altona, MB R0G 0B0
Canada

www.friesenpress.com

ISBN
978-1-03-919556-1 (Hardcover)
978-1-03-919555-4 (Paperback)
978-1-03-919557-8 (eBook)

1. POETRY, CANADIAN

Distributed to the trade by The Ingram Book Company

To two dear friends:

Rejeanne who spurred me on with titles, and

June who was relentless in pushing me to publish

—Thank You—

POEMS FROM THE HEART

Poems from the Heart is a thoughtful collection of poetry categorized into five broad areas: life, love, loss, laughter, and poems straight from the poet's heart.

The book includes both free verse and rhyming poetry that reflects the poet's experiences throughout her life, and her views on our changing world. Written over a short period of time, the poems resonate with thoughts, tragedies, values, and life issues that can impact us all. Many of the poems are based on the experiences of the poet and those she knows as she navigates the life of a mother, wife, and grandmother.

LIFE

Poems Reflecting on Life:

Our Choices

Our Realities

Our Experiences

How Life Might be Seen

A Watchful Eye

What watercolour has taught me
Is to have a watchful eye
Learning how the sun falls, shadows
The mist over the city
How tree trunks bend
How light can create magic

Movement, especially in the sky
Clouds changing formation
Streaks of colour that blend and break
Waves high above
Misty-looking lines falling into each other
And a perfect blue with nothingness around it

Water is another thing, a mystery in itself
It can be still, it can ripple
It can surge, its colours vary
From shore to horizon it can bleed
Its movement can be mesmerizing
It can devastate!

Flowers are intriguing, something to respect
Their colours can't be replicated
They're nature's trophy
They help pollinate the Earth
Painting them is either easy or difficult
Depending on the watchful eye

Then there are the mountains
Dark, cold, and grey rock
Or sun-kissed and shimmering
Depends on the day and the line of sight
Another of nature's colour riddles
They are a difficult canvas for me

Trees can be tricky, watch them closely
They are strikingly beautiful even in dead clusters
Their trunks are all so different
Twisted, straight, scrawny, tall, bent
Their foliage gives them beauty
But even in the dead of winter, they shine!

So have a watchful eye in nature
Its beauty comes in many forms
Watch how light changes its colour and its strength
Always something to focus on
Always keep a watchful eye!
We are surrounded by it, even on our city streets

FORGIVENESS

Forgiveness is a beginning
It's letting go of anger
Lifting your mind
To a better place

Depending on the hurt
The heartache felt
And the sorrow it brought
It can take years

Forgiveness is a journey
To a better place
In your heart and mind
And in your soul

It can lift you up
It can soften the edge
It can bring light forward
It can be salvation

Choices

In childhood we learn
How to make choices
Ice cream or cookie
Red, yellow, or blue
This toy or that toy

As we grow it's harder
This friend or that friend
Brown, black, or white
Not quite there yet
Knowing just to pick the friend *you* like

As teens it's even harder
Too many choices
Too many conflicts
Too much of life's turmoil
Sometimes the choices are not good

As life settles we've learned
Consequences!
We appreciate compromises
But we still make
Mistakes!

Life goes on
We succeed and fail
In relationships, careers, family
We understand our choices
But did we make the right ones?

As we age we question
Life's choices
A pointless quest, really
We can't change the past
We need to appreciate the whys

Choices are fleeting
They sometimes haunt
They also bring joy
Bring laughter
Bring peace

Appreciate the right ones
—Discard the rest—

WORRY

It is a very well-known fact
That women worry more than men
Their thoughts are so distracting
And their reasons never end

Worry doesn't do the trick
It doesn't help a bit
It only serves to agitate
To that we won't admit

With worry comes anxiety
And it does not take away
Whatever might just happen
Those worries they just stay

Or maybe by some miracle
The worries that are near
Just disappear all on their own
They never were to fear

Worry starts with thinking
But not of all things good
It comes from speculation
Of what we might or should

Perhaps tomorrow's worries
Simply need to cease
Just so we can hold onto
Today's most perfect peace

Hope for the Best
Prepare for the Worst*

It's 2023 now
And the world is really screwed
Don't know what to blame it on
Seems something's very skewed

For reasons still unknown to me
The human brain has morphed
Into a form of mystery
A sense of last resort

Logic's left this world of ours
The homeless roam our streets
Poverty surrounds us
And history now repeats

Wars galore, starvation
Common sense is gone
Our youth have trouble focusing
And feel they don't belong

Those of us who will believe
We're smarter than the rest
Still can't keep our system straight
It's pathetic at its best

So always hope for the very best
Cause this world is truly cursed
But be prepared for anything
Prepare for the very worst!

—ALWAYS—

LIFE IS FRAGILE*

There are those born with a lost soul
Not sure who they really are
Not understanding why they feel different
Wanting something else, but
Simply not sure what

There are those born different
Lacking in some ways
And not even knowing it
Happy in themselves or in their simplicity
So what do they really lack

There are those born with all advantages
Who struggle through life
Lack happiness, direction, fortitude
No tolerance for life or others
They are lost to the world

There are those born with opportunity
Some grasp hold and find their way
Others simply can't quite see the light
They might lead a reasonable life
But they all won't find happiness

There are those born in poverty
Who somehow find the strength to succeed
To do better, to work harder
To overcome obstacles they face
They find a stable path

There are those born to love only themselves
Who simply don't see others
Whose greed shines in their eyes
They disrespect perceived differences
And lack foresight and thoughtfulness

We are all born to the same world
Some of us can find the strength to survive
Others struggle with life's challenges
Some become leaders and some flounder all the way
BUT no one of us is better than any of the others

—LIFE IS FRAGILE SO LIVE IT WELL—

Imagine a World

Imagine a world
Where the colour of my skin
The curl of my hair
The scar on my face
My hearing impairment
My glasses, my race
Didn't matter

Imagine a world
Where all children had food
The homeless had homes
The sick all had care
The needy were safe
Elections were fair
Amazing world

Imagine a world
Where flooding and earthquakes
Tornados and storms
Fires in forests
Are all not the norm
Remember?

Imagine a world
Where war was now peace
Tyrants and despots
War mongers, oppressors
Those without heart
The world of aggressors
All gone

Imagine a world
Where we take baby steps
To fix the parts we can
To look each other in the eye
Do one small thing
Let's give it a try
Maybe

—But I still can't imagine—

LIFE IS ON A WAITING LIST

I have no patience for many things
Line ups are the worst
Hurry up and wait my friend
I'm never, ever first

Wait for appointments—what's the point
A time has been reserved
But still I'm sitting anxiously
Will I ever just be served

Wait for tickets bought online
At the mercy of the game
Hours pass as I try my best
But it's a failure just the same

Wait for the school bus—gorgeous day
But it's later than the norm
Standing in a heavy wind
And there is no perfect storm

Waiting for a surgery
Who would ever think
That I would wait for hours
For a biscuit and a drink

Waiting for decisions
From our government so wrong
Only to be finally told
That a study must be done

Waiting for a phone call
From a doctor or a bank
Can't leave the house for anything
Onto the couch I sank

Waiting for the sun to rise
Or wanting it to set
Waiting for the day to start
Wishing I'd forget

Waiting's now a way of life
The lines they stretch afar
Life is on a waiting list
And results are just bizarre!

Books are Powerful

Books in their cases
A few on the floor
Hiding on shelves
Some at my door

Grab one and read
A whodunnit or two
Fiction, non-fiction
A political coup!

There's science and health
Humour and history
Travel and art
Poetry and mystery

No matter your choices
A book can give peace
A place to walk into
You'll feel the release

Just find a space
A big cozy chair
A chaise in the sunshine
But reader beware

That book can take you
To places unknown
Finding friends, foes
And secret zones

Enjoy every book
And the space that you choose
Don't worry if sometimes
You happen to snooze!

Books are Powerful!
—Read on—

A Summer Day

The sound of the tree frogs
And crickets in the heat
The colours of my garden
With flowers smelling sweet

Feet up on a lounge chair
Grandkids in the pool
An icy drink beside me
To help keep me cool

Surrounded by my spruce trees
The maples, birches, pines
Dinner on the barbecue
Perhaps a glass of wine

Our lawn is thick and healthy
A lovely kind of green
With children's toys all over it
A perfect summer scene

Then into the evening
The children, they are gone
We sit together quietly
Enjoying evening's song

The Power of the Sun

A morning sun peeks up and rises over time
A blinding blaze of colour
And then it slowly fades
As day moves on it comes and goes
Obscured behind the clouds
The warmth it brings in winter
Is welcome to the soul

But summer sun can 'melt' me
Too hot, it makes me hide
'Til the evening sun starts falling
But its heat remains behind
Pleasant heat, the kind we need
On a lovely summer eve
Just enough to make me smile
With its promise to return

In fall and spring it's different
It peeks about all day
Sometimes hiding, sometimes not
And with a cooler blaze
But always welcome, always glad
To see it rise above
We need our sun to make us feel
That life will be okay

Sights Unseen

Children born without sight
See things a different way
They even have to learn
A different kind of play

Being born without vision
Is a challenge in itself
But to be born with sight and lose it
Is really something else

Those with sight can never know
What blindness is about
We take for granted what we have
But what if you're without

Think on that for seconds
Close your eyes and contemplate
Let your senses kick right in
Now feel the heavy weight

Imagine how your life would change
The learning curve ahead
The things you can and cannot do
The fear, the loss, the dread

Now think back on those children
Who start their life that way
A learning curve so different
Never to see the light of day

Be thankful if you have your sight
Take care, protect and hope
That nothing untoward takes place
Since sight is no one's joke!

SNOW

Like salt being sprinkled on the earth
Barely visible until the wind moves it
Gathering power the flakes grow
A light dusting covers the ground
It's just a bit of snow

As time moves on, the flakes grow
It's beautiful to watch
Tumbling happily to the ground
And building higher as it falls
It's just a snowy day

Now piling higher, but easing up
On it goes for hours
The wind creates the drifts
The trees are covered, boughs drooping
It's just a magnificent sight

Ploughs, blowers, and shovels emerge
Neighbours helping neighbours
Children's laughter everywhere
They're bundled up to play
It's just the sounds of winter

Footprints everywhere and angels too
A snowman on the lawn
Not so beautiful anymore! Or is it?
Children's laughter, rosy cheeks
It's just winter at its best

The Blanket

Knitted with love
Gifted to baby
Warm and soft
Held in little fingers
Laying on floor
Baby is playing
Dragged by the toddler
Stuffy wrapped in it
Washed umpteen times
To bed with the child
Folded up nicely
Placed in a drawer
Child has found it
Now on the couch
Cuddled and cozy
Four-year old hugs it
Closes her eyes
Napping with blankly
Refolded by child
Back in the drawer
'Til next time!

The Magic of a Child

Children can be difficult
Cantankerous and mean
They can run you into madness
And make a public scene

They can also be so wonderful
With smiles and laughs and noise
Imagination fills their day
While playing with their toys

They say the most amazing things
Be careful what you say
For some of it might come right back
And ruin your lovely day

Their minds are little sponges
They watch and learn and seek
Surprising us with what they know
And how articulate their speech

But the greatest thing with children
Is the love they show to us
Their hugs and cuddles bring a smile
Their presence is a plus

Enjoy them every minute
As they grow so very fast
Although they'll always love you
This dynamic does not last

LOVE

Poems Reflecting:

The Love of

Life, Family, Friendship

Things We Carry in our Hearts

A Special Friendship

There are seven women
So very close to me
In wonderful ways
We usually do agree

Together a long time
Our friendship abounds
We seem always able
To find common ground

When one of us suffers
We're never without
As far as the distance
That's what it's about

If push came to shove
And one needed their aid
They'd all come together
They'd not be afraid

Whether written in words
Or just over a chat
Or magically meeting
We can all count on that

These beautiful women
Bring laughter and more
It's a friendship forever
With amazing candour
—And love—

—A Friendship Forever—

LOST SPIRIT

It seemed to come on suddenly
But in retrospect, said, *"No!"*
It consumed their mind and spirit
They struck their lowest low

This devil in them flourished
Building up as time went by
The person that we knew and loved
We couldn't figure why

This affliction, it is terrible
The person can't decide
Who to trust, and who not
They seek a place to hide

Fear takes hold of everything
The windows in their home
Deceit and terror follow them
They feel so much alone

They isolate inside their home
For days without a word
Not understanding what they caused
The sense of family blurred

A very big mistake took place
They couldn't face the truth
They blamed so many others
It was easy and it soothed

From here we do not know the end
They have to seek to change
Gain control of life itself
Not falter to deranged

Only time and family love
Might help them crawl back out
But we're not sure they're strong enough
To trust and banish doubt

HOPE AND FAITH*

"Hope springs eternal"
That's what Alexander Pope wrote
The meaning sometimes escapes us
It implies that we can hope
Into eternity

Sometimes hope needs faith
As deep inside we know
That the hope we have
Cannot be eternal
But faith adds a new dynamic

Faith implies confidence
Confidence in a plan
In a human being
In our desire for
A positive outcome

Hope and faith together
Can bring relief from anxiety
Can keep us grounded
Can bring some peace
Where otherwise there might be none

Hope and faith live side by side
In order for them to be successful
They need for us
To believe a wish will come true
A desire will be successful

Hope and Faith
—Carry them in your Heart—

KINDNESS

Kindness
"Friendly, generous, considerate"
That definition's true
But why is it so difficult
For all of us to do

We're kind to those
We truly love
But not so kind to strangers
It's hard for us to see their face
Since all we see is danger

Danger of what?
Perceived or true
It's hard to figure out
These are humans just like us
Of that there is no doubt

Because my friend
The world has changed
Before our very eyes
Afraid to even walk our streets
As crime is on the rise

We walk on by
We close our eyes
Even for a second
Just to make us feel good
Pretend—is what I reckon

So let us all
Rethink what's kind
What small things we can do
To make this world a better place
A 'kindness to others' debut!

Kindness to people
Or all of God's creatures
Kindness to ourselves
Any little gesture
Whatever your kindness compels

Music To My Ears

The sultry sounds of waves on shore
Soothing to my heart
It calms my fears
It slows my breath
It's music to my ears

Waves on warm and sunny days
Crashing on the beach
They bring to light
The vulnerable
And the very weak

Tickling gently as I walk
Along the sandy beach
My thoughts begin to lighten
My skin is warm
My mind is now at peace

I walk into the water
And it splashes up my legs
Cool and oh so glorious
I catch an
ocean breeze

I listen now so carefully
The sounds the ocean brings
A booming wash
But calming
It makes my heart just sing

And if you find that perfect beach
Where solitude surrounds
Your spirit
Will feel lightened
Your soul will settle down

So sing the praise
To sand and surf
To solitude and peace
Soothe the heart, heal the soul
Be grateful for release

—Just feel it!—

PLEASURE

What brings me pleasure
May not please you
I love the coolness of a summer breeze
And winter's fine sunshine
The snow on the trees

You love the heat
A seaside resort
With palm trees and sand
A winter vacation
Your skin warm and tanned

Pleasure is not about anyone else
It's what makes you happy
That's what it's about
A form of delight and gratification
Something that humans can't go without

Pleasure can be as simple as food
Chocolate and Truffles
A great piece of meat
Lobster and oysters
A raspberry sweet

Pleasure's a feeling
From the love of a partner
Great boisterous laughter
Time with good friends
A home to look after

Pleasure is something
We need to seek out
It helps us through harder days
It puts a smile upon our face
And gives a push to fight malaise

So when you feel you need a lift
Find something that you love
A person, place, just anything
That pleasures you a lot
You'll be surprised what love can bring

—Pleasure on—

FOR THE LOVE OF SIGHT & SOUND

When born with sight
And sounds abound
We take for granted
What surrounds

We move through life
So unaware
That all life's beauty
Is everywhere

We hear the songs
Of wind and birds
We see so much
We read the words

Little thought is ever given
To losing sound or sight
Hearing nothing
Losing light

So much in life
We value lightly
Until one day
We lose it slightly

Or maybe even more is lost
All our sights and sounds
Have we stored them safely?
Can they still be found?

So let us with our sound and sight
Store it all away
In case one day we lose it
And loss does not betray

Enjoy the sounds
Sweet songs and cackles
Cherish the sights
Blue jays and grackles

The sound of a storm
The sway of a tree
"All creatures great and small"
And the roaring of the sea

Take not for granted
Sound and sight
Bless these gifts
They shine so bright!

A MOTHER'S LOVE

Not something every mother has
But most cannot release
That special love they carry
And it never does decrease

Regardless of successes
Our children sometimes fail
For reasons we might know or not
Their fight's to no avail

It may be sickness growing
Addiction is a cause
But a mother cannot let them go
There's only time for pause

Take a moment, pick them up
Bring them home for care
Hope they find the strength within
But this is often rare

As time goes on and things don't change
The mother still has hope
That they will find the strength within
And learn a way to cope

And when they don't, exhaustion hits
The mother suffers too
She has no life within her
And her world has gone askew

Tough love is often bantered
From those who watch the fight
But if mothers' love is always there
Tough love seems just not right

An endless fight that wears so deep
A mother's love can break
But deep within it never ends
She knows exactly what's at stake

So if you know a mother
Who can't give up the fight
Don't judge her chosen reasons
Support her in her plight

WHAT IS A FRIEND?

What is a Friend?
A confidant who listens
Remembers your woes
Talks you through hard times
But never dismisses, simply listens

What is a Friend?
A person who can make you smile
Make you chuckle
Gives the very best of medicines
That belly roaring laugh!

What is a Friend?
Someone who is there
Through good times and bad
Through life's hardest moments
Through life's very best

What is a Friend?
Someone whose hugs are memorable
Whose touch makes a difference
Whose smile turns tears to laughter
Whose thoughts matter to you

What is a Friend?
A person you love
A person you trust
A person you respect
A person just like *you*!

LOSS

Poems Reflecting:

The Loss of Life

The Loss of Ourselves

The Loss of Hope

Sorrow Felt

Ukrainian Tragedy

Tragedy is happening
The world does seem to care
But no one seems quite able
To find solutions there

When war breaks out around us
We tend to close our eyes
As everything about it
Is too visual to disguise

We know it's wrong, we see the pain
Our hearts go out to all
The beauty of the country's gone
As we watch its cities fall

But evil's in the making
With a monster at its head
We pray for all the children
And mourn the country's dead

Some of his own soldiers
Don't understand the fight
Didn't know the enemy
And hope it turns out right

The world around us watches
Prayers go out to *stop*
A democratic country
From becoming
A Russian bleeding spot

—God save Ukraine—

IF ONLY

If only I had done this
If only I had not
If only I had thought it through
If only I had fought

Fought the fears deciding brings
Made a different choice
Decided not to do it
Used a different voice

The ifs can drive you crazy
Make life so hard to bear
Sleep becomes so fleeting
As you melt into despair

Blame is all encompassing
Your brain cannot digest
All the ifs and whatnots
Brings you total stress

There are no wrong decisions
They're made with what you know
Hindsight's not forgiving
You need to let it go!

If only I had done this
If only I had not
Serves no real purpose
A useless, painful thought

And So it Goes*

Life is filled with challenges
We did and did not choose
We either venture forward
Or surely we will lose

Lose what, you ask—I'll tell you now
You'll lose yourself for sure
And this is simply how you will
For this there is no cure

You'll blame yourself or self-indulge
Or cry and hurt and pout
You'll wish that things were different
You'll fill yourself with doubt

And worse than that you'll find a way
To search and find great fear
In every aspect of your day
Your mind will not be clear

Fear of laughter, fear of fun
Fear of phones and texts
Fear of loving, life and death
Wondering what comes next

So take the challenges given you
Enjoy each day ahead
Look for laughter, look for fun
Banish all that dread

Life goes on despite our frets
Control does not exist
Rest your mind and fill your heart
Find peace, it will assist!

—And so it goes—

COVID

COVID is a killer
A killer of the body and of the mind
Over time it has been a killer of the spirit
It has changed the world

When its ugly head first appeared
We all hunkered down
Knowing, full well, that it would end
But, sadly, it did not

Scientists and doctors and politicians
Told us what they knew, or did they?
Tragically, they knew very little
And even less as time went by

And it went by slowly
It brought loneliness and boredom
It vanished us from family and friends
It smothered us unmercifully

Brief moments in time brought relief
Outdoor visits, hugging with masks
Restaurants open, friends together
But always, always with caution

Then new strains emerged
Shut down, hunker down, feel down
Senior hour grocery shopping
New recipes, reading, crafting

Anything to keep our sanity
But the loneliness and despair persisted
The lucky ones had a 'bubble'
Consistent people they could count on

Even the 'bubble' could not erase
The loneliness, the fear, the absence of hope
And it went on and on and on
Rendering a tragic split in the world we knew

COVID is and will forever be
A piece of this world's history

A Canadian Loss

Humbolt and Dauphin
The young and the old
Horrendous collisions
With stories untold

Roads integrate
Vehicles collide
Hard to believe
Nowhere to hide

The process itself
Determines the cause
But cause will not matter
To those who have lost

Children and parents
Loved ones and friends
People who knew them
Memories don't end

Only time will give peace
To communities suffering
But nothing brings back
It leaves our minds wondering

What if they weren't
In the bus or the truck
What if three seconds
Changed everyone's luck

Tragedy strikes
When it's least expected
Healing takes years
For those affected

No words can describe
The pain and regret
Only time will heal
But we'll never forget

DESPAIR

It starts with overthinking
Overreacting
Maybe even overdoing
Its cause is peripheral
But the feelings are real
And can last very long

It quickly turns to worry
About what, you might ask?
About a sick family member
About your own health
About infidelity or work
About almost anything

Despair has no boundaries
It eats you up
It hides deep inside
Until something is resolved
Determined to be true or false
Settled in your mind

Death brings despair
Let good memories heal the loss
Our health can bring despair
Fight for it with all your might
Infidelity brings despair
Accept it, leave it, or repair it

Despair can't heal
It's up to you to make that happen
Almost like the addict
One day at a time
Look for solutions
Find yourself again

LOST

It came from a darkness
That no one could see
It haunted my heart
And it tormented me

I tried to climb out
On a dull winter day
But my spirit just held me
And shut me away

The sun shone brightly
But I still felt despair
No one could help me
Despite how they cared

A sadness surrounds me
I cannot explain
I feel like I'm standing
In a down-pouring rain

These feelings of mine
They come and they go
Sometimes they're short
And sometimes not so

Why is this torture
Focused on me
Why can't happiness
Simply be

The people around me
Are lost—what to do?
I need to do something
I *need* to pull through

EMPTY

Life can sometime feel so strange
Empty is the word
Perhaps we're bored
Or something's gone
That leaves us feeling
Just absurd

It comes from deep inside of us
A very private threat
No rhyme or reason to it
A loss of something
Hard to pin
Or something to regret

Empty of emotion
No hand or heart to hold
Feelings buried
Deep inside
Emptiness profound
Our spirit feels so cold

It's not depression or malaise
It's not loss or fear
It's a hollowness
That drains the mind
Drowns the heart
And makes demons reappear

We need to look deep inside
Find something good to do
Get out from
underneath it all
Kill the endless void
And take a different view

Easy said, but hard to do
Half empty or half full
Find a way to fill your heart
To love yourself
Dig deep inside
Feel the pleasant pull

HATE

There is no place
In life for hate
It breeds antipathy
It builds like fire
It burns intense
It unmercifully inspires

Hate from one
Breeds hate to many
Taking little time
Before too long
Your world has changed
Hate runs deep and strong

Hate your neighbour
Hate your town
Hate who governs you
Hate yourself
Hate the world
Hate sustains itself

Hate is sometimes fired
By a consequence of fear
Or simply by exposure
To jealousy and dread
By listening to others
Who get deep into your head

Hate can bring on tragedy
Strong voices then strong acts
Then terror reins, lives collapse
All we know is gone
Our world can change before our eyes
But hate will carry on!

—Hate is such a worthless and evil energy—

Our Earth

Given to us free of charge
Free of pollution, clean water
Streams and waterfalls unchanged
Except by the Earth itself

It was populated by man and beast
For more years than the mind can imagine
It is still populated by man and beast
But its changes are startling!

Humans have managed the Earth
Over time with little care
The value placed on our Earth
Has diminished to greed

Greed for profit, ownership, demand
We concede to what we think we need
Regardless of what it does
To this great Earth

Recycle, reuse, are myths in reality
As much as we think we're trying
We're really just hiding it all
And harming man and beast in the process

It seems there are no solutions
But, in reality, man does not want
To see the reality, find the solutions
And beast cannot help us

When I leave this Earth
My greatest regret will be that I have surely
Contributed to the Earth I leave behind
For my grandchildren to live on

—I wish I could have done better—

Rain and Water

Rain is unpredictable
Even by the best
It can come down in torrents
It can be gentle
It can devastate

It can touch you softly
While swimming in a pool
It can give relief from the blazing sun
It can last for minutes, even seconds
It waters our gardens

Rain can start slowly
Then get heavier and heavier
It can be accompanied by
Thunder and lightening
And high winds

It can be relentless
Day after miserable day
Tormenting
Flooding homes and streets
Over-banking rivers and oceans

Rain can kill
People and animals
It can damage vegetation
And farmland
It can harm our earth

But without it
Where would our world be?
Water is a source of life
Water is necessary for our survival
Water can be a saviour

If we save our Earth
We can save our water
If we kill our Earth
Water will likely kill us
Consider the options!

Sorrow

Sorrow is a sadness
That our hearts cannot suppress
It's found so deep inside us
And causes such distress

Sorrow is a loss within
That cannot be described
It's a crushing blow, a gut ache
The emotion can't be denied

It drives our feelings inward
The loss is so profound
That nothing takes the pain away
Because heartache knows no bounds

They tell us time will heal all things
They tell us to be strong
But when you feel the depth of loss
You know that they are wrong

Then one day something happens
Your memories come to life
The good, the bad, the happy times
They seem to curb your strife

Sorrow takes a backbench
The world, it lightens up
You think not of the loss you've had
But rather what you've got

The loss is not forgotten
But the memories, they do thrive
Your sorrow never leaves you
It's what you needed to survive

LAUGHTER

Poems Reflecting:

How Humour Heals

Laughter Keeps Us Sane

And a Wee Bit of Fun

LAUGHTER

Laughter is the spice of life
A saviour of our souls
A therapeutic antidote
To mend our rigid woes

Laughter makes us feel alive
Our mood will be enhanced
It fills us up with wonder
Our minds will be entranced

Your lungs will feel wide open
Your breathing will improve
You might be quite surprised
How your joints—they start to move

Depression will fade faster
As your belly laugh does grow
Relief will fill you up at once
You'll feel it to your toes

A boost to your whole system
Immunity will strive
Your skin will brighten up a bit
And a smile will fill your eyes

Your heart will feel protected
From the scariest of things
Its blood flow won't be hampered
It's like you've grown wings

Laughter burns up calories
So those who need that help
Can find some reassurance
That improvement will be felt

So please find a reason
To put a smile upon your face
A giggle or a belly laugh
Whatever you embrace

The joy of all great humour
Immeasurable in health
Brings happiness upon us
Unsurpassed by any wealth

—Let me hear it: laughter!—

My Head is Fully Furnished*

My head is fully furnished
And I need the used stuff gone
Most of it is out of date
And it does not belong

It's taking up too much space
My brain cannot accept
This stuff is even needed
I'll dump it with no regrets

Some of it my parents left
And that was long ago
The good things I'll remember
The rest I can just throw

Regrets that I have stored for life
Can move on with the rest
No point in keeping things like that
They only add to stress

The loss of lives can go as well
Remember all that's dear
Storing loss is useless
If good memories still run clear

What else can I dispense with
The things that cause me tears
Worry, fear, and anger
Can all but disappear

My head is feeling better now
Lighter and not as tense
It's nice to feel lifted
Cause the stuff has been condensed

If your head is fully furnished
And the old stuff has to go
Order up the dump truck
And begin the mighty throw!

Laughter Through Tragedy*

Through life's many tragedies
Sadness can abound
But find yourself a special friend
Where solace can be found

A conversation starts
With facts, insights, and tears
And as discussion deepens
It starts dissolving fears

Friends who listen mean so much
No judgement in their voice
No blame, no hurt, no fault is found
Results begin by choice

Choosing to find laughter
As there's always some to find
Maybe from your friendship past
Or something deep inside

Laughter is a healer
It puts tragedy aside
If even for a moment
Let laughter be your guide

It soothes the soul, brings a smile
And softens all the pain
It makes us think much clearer
Laughter helps to keep us sane

Restring My Life*

The strings on my pearls broke today
So off to the jeweller I went
I simply asked, can you restring this strand
Cause I have an upcoming event

I sure can do that, you lovely young thing
Just leave them here for today
Back I went to pick them up
They're gorgeous is all I could say

Something was broken and then it got fixed
Simplicity struck at its best
A few bucks later they're better than new
If life was this simple, I'd never feel stressed

I wandered on home, wearing my pearls
And I suddenly thought oh, how nice
If my troubles and worries and tears could all go
And I could simply RESTRING my whole life!

THE CHIPMUNKS AND THE POOL

I look out back and there it is
A chipmunk trying to swim
It must be spring and it's very young
Just jumped in on a whim

I rush outside and grab the scoop
His swimming is not bad
But we all know his strength is low
With no help, the results will be sad

I dump him gently on the ground
He shivers and he shakes
Then knows it's time to find his home
And runs with all it takes

This scene is not the only one
It happens all the time
The baby chipmunks play like kids
From water they can't climb

So there I am with watchful eye
Just looking out the door
My trusty scoop awaits me
It's just another chore!

Spring in Ontario

Dirty snow and rainy days
Sometimes even ice
Temps will rise and then they'll fall
It really is not nice

Creatures they all venture out
Not sure if spring is here
The birds fly north to make their nests
Their tenacity I revere

The bears in the wild lift dozy heads
And start to leave their dens
Relentless in their search for food
They eat to their hearts' content

The crocus, tulips, and daffodils
Peek out from the earth above
Some reaching through a snowy patch
It's almost a labour of love

Love for the sun that breaks through the cloud
Love for the springtime rain
All living creatures venture forth
For us humans it keeps us sane

The honking of geese might be a first sign
That spring is almost here
But don't be surprised by a wee bit of snow
It can bring back a feeling of fear

Fear that the flowers will wither on cue
Fear that the sun will not shine
Fear that the birds will stop singing
And fear that the stars won't align

But put that fear aside my friend
Spring is here to stay
It's just where we live, it's a season
That's changeable day by day

The sun will shine, the rain will fall
The temperatures will improve
And sooner than you'd ever think
You'll be in a summer groove!

—Thank goodness for summer in Ontario!—

THE COVEN

A group of women gather
With intent to have some fun
Libation does surround them
And their day has just begun

They call themselves the Coven
You know, witches with their brooms
And they talk about the cauldron
But trepidation looms

They could have googled cauldron
And found out what to do
But they'd rather gather playfully
And they haven't got a clue

So they sit around and chat it up
About life and love and sex
They toast with their tequila
And decide what should come next

Over time they've done some crazy things
But always landed well
Even on that cruise ship
Oh, those stories we can't tell

This Coven has existed
For many, many years
And now all eight are seniors
Raise a glass and just say *cheers*!

But never disregard them
Surprises they abound
Be careful what you say to them
Their potions can confound

A group of crazy seniors
No definition plays
But watch out for that cauldron
One day it might just blaze!

ENTERTAINING

I must have walked 10,000 steps
And that I will regret
Then climbing up and down those stairs
My back is screaming, then I sweat!

I've made the cookies, cake, and pie
The meatballs are a go
Potatoes have been readied
I've even shovelled snow!

The bread is in the oven
How wondrous it does smell
I'm sitting on my ass right now
'Till the oven rings its bell

Two bathrooms and three toilets
Still to clean today
Then vacuum in the morning
So their dogs can run and play

The table needs to pretty up
The chickens need to thaw
And people need to bring their things
And make sure they're not raw!

I'm older now and this is hard
But kids don't get the point
I love them all to pieces
But they do not have my joints

This entertaining 'thing' I do
Just needs to go away
Or I just need to use my words
"No thank you", I should say

I'm sure in time they'll get it
And see I'm lacking speed
But maybe I should burn the food (hm!)
And then they might accede!

So now I think I'll have my wine
A glass or two is good
Might make me sit upon my ass
Forget about 'what should'!

Hosting

Hosting is an art
That many do not sport
The art of making guests at home
Their attempts fall very short

When you arrive you bring your stuff
Yes, all of it I fear
Pillows, sheets, and blankets
And, yes, your case of beer

You wait for dinner to be served
Don't hold your breath for long
Cause that ain't gonna happen
Unless I'm really wrong

Just get up off your butt, sweet thing
And head on to the kitchen
If luck isn't on your side
You'll need to take to witching

Open up that fridge and pray
There's food that you can cook
While the hostess sits upon a chair
Enjoying her new book

Chatting away, merrily
All about herself
Sipping on the wine you brought
While you cook with no one's help

Then after dinner, have a beer
Or maybe two or three
Toddle off to make your bed
Then clean up the debris

If you're really lucky
You'll pack up quick
Escape that place forever
But don't be really ticked

Some people only see themselves
No thought to others' needs
And hosting never crossed their path
Be happy you have speed

Amble off, be very fast
And never go back there
Be glad that you are leaving
And please, do not despair

You know what hosting's all about
Treat guests like they are king
Make them feel right at home
And they need not bring a thing!

GROWING OLD

Did that just happen
I ask myself
As I look into a mirror
Oh Lord I don't remember
When my face turned into
My mother!

It happened oh so suddenly
The body creaks and aches
The skin turned crepey
Overnight
The boobs fell to my knees
Very scary!

My memory
Where did it go?
As I stare right at the stove
Forgot what I was looking for
But I'm sure it's not in there
Try the fridge!

Where on Earth are my keys
I've lost them more than once
I open drawers
I check the coats
I trudge from room to room
In my hand!

The chores I used to do
With ease
Get harder every day
Do I really need to dust the house?
Can't write my name just yet
Feet up!

It all came on so suddenly
This aging thing
I've got!
Good thing I still remember
Where I store my favourite
Wine!

Men/Women

Men and women differ
Extremely so I fear
Men can't find 'it' on a shelf
Unless, of course, it's beer!

Women see in detail
Each item on that shelf
They have no problem finding things
They need no man to help

Men have friends and friendships
But the candour isn't strong
Feelings aren't a topic
They see that as just wrong

Women have strong friendships
No barriers apply
They share, chat, and giggle
And maybe even cry

Men tend to bottle up
Emotions buried deep
They keep too much inside of them
But often still find sleep

Women want to let it out
In talk and anger too
Put it on the table
Share their point of view

But men can be so loving
Helpful, sweet, and kind
And women can appreciate
Their special states of mind!

Thank goodness we can make it work
Or where would we all be
A world without compromise
Would be a world where we'd agree!

—No thanks—

FROM MY HEART

Poems Reflecting:

Some Very Personal Thoughts

Of and About the Poet

Writing Poems

My thoughts are flowing
From my mind
Creating poems
Of every kind

There is no
Reason for this trend
No why or wherefore
I can pen

Today I've written
Four fine prose
With little hardship
As it goes

From fun
To visions in my head
It seems to be
My mission said

Creating poetry
Day by day
Regardless of what
My words convey

So please enjoy
As you read
A laugh, a cry
An emotional need

Whatever pleasure
You can find
Whatever helps your
State of mind

COMFORT

No bigger than the palm of my hand
A puppy came to stay
A tiny little creature
Whose paws would soon betray

She grew up very quickly
With a gorgeous chocolate coat
Bigger than we thought she would
And a character to note

She loved to lick her people
A way to show her love
She had a few fine nicknames
Lady Lick-a-lot—it won!

Cera was our chocolate lab
Not the smartest beast
But a heart that reached to everyone
And she loved a boney feast

She always walked with nose to ground
Her favourite boy along
We were only afterthoughts
Unless the boy was gone

She lived a long and healthy life
A water dog at heart
Fifteen years of loving her
Her passing was so hard

No other dog could comfort
The way that Cera could
We'll always have great memories
Of a dog that was so good

We have a remembrance garden rock
That is so very cleaver
"If love could have saved you
You would have lived forever"

TRAVEL

I've travelled less than many
And more than enough
I've seen the beauty of this Earth
I know its value—what travel's worth

It opens your mind to see things anew
To respect all our differences
Appreciate our past
Answers many questions asked

I've seen fjords and the Baltic Sea
I've seen Scandinavia in all its beauty
Some of the world's most amazing sights
And the beauty of the darkest nights

I've seen my country from east to west
With a beauty that never fails me
Mountains, prairies, farmlands, and more
A glorious country from shore to shore

I've seen islands in the sunny south
Much of the States and so much more
Mexico, Bermuda, Eastonia as well
The good, the bad, and lots to tell

Travel gets harder as we age
It's a chore to pack the bag
And the world we know has surely changed
But its mysteries can keep us fully engaged

So travel if and when you can
Enjoy every moment
Savour it all wherever you are
It doesn't matter—near or far

Let travel show you things unknown
Open your mind, change your tune
Meet new people and even new friends
Enjoy every moment, see how it ends!

My World

I grew up in a world
Where I was seen and not heard
My voice it was stifled
Do not say a word!

But that didn't stop me
From using my head
From listening and learning
And watching instead

As a child I might cower
Afraid to say boo
Did my chores and homework
Then retreated quietly to my room

As a teen I got rowdy
I found my own voice
I defied what they told me
I learned I had choice

As I entered the workforce
I saw what *she* feared
Men who had power
Who felt so revered

In their ties and their suits
With their know-it-all sense
My presence around them
Reared their defence

My *mother* had given me
Her sense of fear
But my father had told me
Stand tall and no tears

Show them you're smart
Show them you can
Show you're determined
But don't show them your plan!

Respect the trustworthy
And the ones who help you
Be cautious of others
And you'll make it through

My father's advice helped me
Through good and through bad
And I made it in business
Thanks to my Dad!

I Never Said

I never said I would be anything
I never said I wanted to be anything
I never said I could be anything
Whatever happened, just happened

I was raised in a time
When things were simpler
When life was slower
No computers or tablets or mobile phones

As a kid, I played outside
I walked to the hamlet for mail and milk
I was allowed out 'til after dark with friends
When bored, I was told to read a book!

As a teenager, I went to school
Cared for two younger brothers
Understood my mother's challenges
Did well in high school

As a young adult, I got a job
Then another and another until
I finally settled in a job that interested me
A job where I could learn

There was no appreciation for benefits
No real thoughts for a future
I took on new challenges and I grew
In life, in love, and in work

Today I say I am intelligent
Today I say I have perseverance
Today I say I am successful
Whatever happened, happened because of me

A Loss Remembered

41 years of life never lived
Because you didn't believe
That growing old could be not bad
And so you made me grieve

Although we loved each other
Much time we spent apart
Although we never talked of it
It pulled on my young heart

You left me once for someone else
The lies, the tears, no truth
And then we reconciled
It may have been our youth

But sadness always followed you
You laughed when it was right
You put a good face forward
Yet it haunted you at night

Your father didn't help you
His head deep in the sand
Even though I begged him
To give a helping hand

It's taken years for me to see
The pain that was within
And understand your need
To end and not begin

I think our souls recycle
A belief that is my own
But I know when you return to life
Your soul, it will have grown

It's taken me so many years
To put my thoughts to pen
Still hard for me to fathom
What happened way back then

You Simply Loved Me

When I was little
You held me close, kept me warm
Helped me learn, played with me
Walked me in my stroller
—You simply loved me—

As a teen you helped me
To find my way in life
Understand our father's death
Our mother's exhaustion
—You simply loved me—

When we took our trip to Scandinavia
You tolerated my youth when I was less than kind
We had a great trip together
Many laughs, lots of memories
—You simply loved me—

As we met life partners
Had families of our own
Held our mother's hand together
When she was dying
—You simply loved me—

When we collided on life issues
You were kind enough to move on
Leave the topic alone
Find other things to talk about
—You simply loved me—

I have 70 years of sisterhood
To thank you for
Being by my side
Whenever I needed you

—Thank you for simply loving me—

A TRAVESTY OF FOOLS

What is a travesty?
A comedy of fools?
A cheap imitation
Of competence and pride
The whole situation
Can hardly be described

Things went wrong
That never should have
Couldn't be fixed
And it's just not right
The patient had to cower
Or they might have lost their sight

Infection sets in
But it's not their fault
Blame it on anyone
It's easy if they try
Even for a doctor
Things can go awry

—I never knew—

That sight could become
A travesty of fools
That the system is damaged
Communication lost
Can't even make appointments
That aren't already botched!

The patient had to understand
How to play their game
But if you fail to do so
The outcome might be worse
It took all I had
Not to repeatedly—just curse!

All said and done
I know in my heart
The system is *broken*
But I did not lose
I simply survived
A Travesty of Fools!

FRIENDSHIP

Friendship can be fleeting
Or last forever more
Ours just keeps on going
It's like an open door

You are a friend who makes me laugh
We chat a mighty storm
You pick me up if I feel down
And leave me feeling warm

This note is here to tell you
I'm thankful you're my friend
Our years together tells me
On you I can depend

WISHING YOU

A day filled with happiness
A world that's at peace
A quiet place to read your book
Some very special treats

Find time to put your feet up
Good health, good times, good fun
Wishing you a year ahead
That's a perfect peaceful one

Flowers on your table
Take a lovely ride
Sunshine in your window
A friend or lover by your side

So have a day that's special
Enjoy what makes you smile
Remember what's important
And do it all in style!

Printed in the USA
CPSIA information can be obtained
at www.ICGtesting.com
LVHW061602060324
773408LV00004BA/8